Original title:
Fernweh in the Forest

Copyright © 2025 Creative Arts Management OÜ
All rights reserved.

Author: Nolan Kingsley
ISBN HARDBACK: 978-1-80566-654-7
ISBN PAPERBACK: 978-1-80566-939-5

## Tales Spun in the Canopy's Embrace

In the trees where squirrels play,
Little jests can save the day.
A raccoon dance by moonlight's beam,
Is the forest living in a dream?

When branches twist in awkward glee,
I swear I saw a wobbly tree.
It tumbled down, just like a cat,
Said, "Mind the root, it's where I'm at!"

A badger dressed in stylish shoes,
Strolled through ferns with nothing to lose.
He winked at crows who cawed in awe,
"I'm the best-dressed critter you ever saw!"

So come and sit beneath the leaves,
Where every rustle is sure to tease.
Giggles echo through the wood,
In this realm where all is good.

## Searching for the Soul of the Woods

Oh what a quest through tangled vines,
To find the heart where humor shines.
I asked a fox, he rolled his eyes,
"You're barking up the wrong surprise!"

The mushrooms chuckled, while I tripped,
And on a branch, a parrot quipped,
"If you seek wisdom, you're too late,
Just dance along and love your fate!"

A glade of willows swayed in mirth,
As I pondered on the woods' true worth.
Did the trees just laugh at me?
Or hold their breath to let me be?

So let the laughter guide your way,
Through the maze where shadows play.
In every crack, a giggle blooms,
And joyous whispers fill the glooms.

## Lunchtime Lullabies of the Leaves


Squirrels chatter as they feast,
A picnic spread, a leafy beast.
Cucumbers roll, they call them acorns,
While ants march in, wearing tiny uniforms.

Beneath the roots, a raccoon snores,
Dreaming of snacks behind closed doors.
I nibble crumbs on a mossy seat,
Laughter rings, nature's lunch is sweet.

## The Map Made of Memories

In the canopy, birds scribble a tale,
Of lost socks and an epic snail trail.
We follow paths with giggles and glee,
Chasing shadows, it's all just for free!

Old trees hold secrets, maps worn and torn,
Pinecones whisper of adventures reborn.
Through winding trails and past the old creek,
We find hidden treasures, it's fun we seek.

**Elysian Whispers in the Woods**

Mushrooms dance in a merry line,
Claiming they're stars, trying to shine.
A tree stump proclaims it's a throne for a goat,
While pine needles tickle, they hum a sweet note.

The wind giggles as it rustles the fronds,
Squirrels join in with their cheeky songs.
Nature's parade, oh what a delight,
In this woodland stage, everything feels right.

## Through the Thicket of Dreams

Branches wave like they're saying, 'Hey!'
While I trip over roots that want to play.
A magical fairy shrinks down to tease,
As daisies hold court under whispers of breeze.

The bushes grumble, they're full of good cheer,
Telling tales as we wander near.
Through tangled paths, we laugh and we run,
In this forest of dreams, we're never outdone.

## The Allure of Forgotten Trails

Lost my way but found a flower,
It whispered tales of nature's power.
Tripped on roots, laughed out loud,
The trees agreed, they were so proud.

Squirrels chattered in glee,
Planning a forest-wide jubilee.
Under a log, a party awaits,
With acorns served on leaf plates!

## Evoking the Essence of Wandering Spirits

A grizzly bear in a party hat,
Danced with a raccoon and a fluffy cat.
They spun and twirled, spooked the deer,
Who thought it was Halloween all year!

Mushrooms giggled, swaying near,
While frogs croaked songs, full of cheer.
A ghost floated by, waving hello,
Saying, 'Join the fun, let's put on a show!'

## Echoes in the Mist

Whispers of owls join the fray,
As shadows perform in a moonlit ballet.
Branches bend, tickling the sky,
Even the wind lets out a sigh.

Fog wraps snug like a cozy blanket,
As foxes gather for a woodland banquet.
Grinning mushrooms lend an ear,
While bantering trees cheer with cheer!

## Beyond the Trees, the World Awaits

A rabbit raced, boasting of speed,
But tripped on a log, oh, what a deed!
Laughter erupted, 'Twas quite a sight,
As hedgehogs chuckled, planning their flight.

Out from the brush, a dance floor was found,
With fireflies twinkling, all around.
So, let's cha-cha down the lane,
In this wild forest, joy is our gain!

## Sunlight's Dance on Forest Floor

Sunshine sprinkles with flair,
Dancing through leaves in midair.
Squirrels prance with nutty cheer,
While rabbits hop, no hint of fear.

Beams of gold, a playful tease,
Teasing shadows, swirling with ease.
Mushrooms giggle beneath the trees,
While gentle breezes sing in the breeze.

## The Allure of Whispering Pines

Whispering winds, such gossip sly,
Pines tell secrets as I pass by.
One tree groans, 'A squirrel's my mate!'
While another laughs, 'I hold your fate!'

With every step, I chance a glance,
At dancing ferns that join the dance.
Their floppy fronds sway to the beat,
As I shuffle along, feeling fleet.

## Shadows of Adventure Await

In the thicket, shadows loom,
Chasing dust bunnies, making room.
A raccoon peeks with a sly delight,
As I stumble onto a twig in fright.

The rustle of leaves, I jump in place,
Thinking it's something, I quicken my pace.
But it's just a stick, old and wise,
Laughing at me in disguise.

## A Tapestry of Twisted Branches


Branches weave a curious art,
Knots and twists, each plays a part.
One says, 'I'm a slide for the brave!'
While another proclaims, 'I'm a treetop wave!'

I climb up high, what a tight squeeze,
And feel like a monkey, swinging with ease.
The branches giggle as I flop down,
Who knew adventures wore such a crown?

## Mysteries in the Moss

In the damp and shady glen,
A squirrel steals my sandwich then!
Underneath a mushroom's cap,
I spot a fox take a nap.

A gnome appears, says 'What gives?',
With jokes that make the bog quite live!
The whispers of the trees are sly,
I think I'll leave before they cry.

## Chasing the Lost Light

I chased a glow through thick, green ferns,
Thought it was gold, but 'twas a worm!
It squiggled and giggled as I tripped,
Over roots where my shoe had slipped.

The sun peeked through, a tease indeed,
A raccoon offered me some seed.
I pondered, 'Is this treasure or trash?'
While squirrels conspired with a splash!

## Sylvan Sojourn

Went on a jaunt, oh such delight,
But the deer threw a party that night!
With disco lights on fireflies' tails,
I became their guest as music wails.

They danced and pranced, so spry and free,
While I struggled to find the beat, oh me!
A worm on stage stole the show,
The woodland wonders put on a glow.

## Beneath the Boughs of Mystery

Beneath the branches, secrets loom,
A bear is reading in his room!
With shades and a hat, he looks so cool,
Who knew that bears played by their own rule?

A raccoon writes poems on old bark,
While owls write critiques till after dark.
With laughter ringing all around,
I pondered if trees could be profound.

## Whispers of the Wandering Pines

Amid the trees, I hear a chat,
The squirrels gossip, imagine that!
They speak of nuts and secret trails,
Of yon bark beetles with grand tales.

A rabbit joins, with ears so tall,
He claims he saw a moose, not small!
While owls laugh at what we've said,
'Cause they've seen more from their high bed.

The blooming flowers dance with grace,
They wink at me, then hide their face.
And in this merry woodland spree,
I lose all sense of time — you see!

So here I stand with glee and cheer,
In nature's humor, always near!
With each rustle and playful jest,
I'm sure the woods know how to jest!

## The Call of Untrodden Paths

Off the beaten track, I roam,
But stumble on a deer-shaped gnome!
With twiggy beard and eyes so bright,
He says, 'Wrong turn? Oh, what a sight!'

He offers me a path to take,
I wonder if it's just a fake.
'Follow me,' he grins with glee,
'You'll find the world of mystery!'

A chorus of crickets burst in song,
As the hedgehog hums along so strong.
They say the bushes hold great lore,
If only I could dash, explore!

Yet here I pause and laugh out loud,
This woodland gathering, quite a crowd!
With roots that trip and leaves that sway,
Adventure lives in every spray!

## Echoes Beneath the Canopy

Underneath the leafy dome,
I hear the laughter of a gnome.
He slides down branches, oh so slick,
While mushrooms giggle — oh, what a trick!

A swinging vine calls out my name,
'Come try this! It's not just a game!'
With a whoosh and a swing, I fly,
Straight into bushes — oh my, oh my!

The woodpecker mocks and taps away,
'Another misadventure in the fray?'
But even as I tumble and roll,
I find new joy, that's my goal!

With echoes of laughter all around,
This forest teaches fun can be found.
In every stumble, twist, and shout,
I see the woodland's playful pout!

## Dreams of Dappled Sunlight

Sunbeams flicker through the trees,
I stretch and catch a light warm breeze.
A lizard blinks, then gives a wink,
I swear he knows more than I think!

The path is bright, but full of bumps,
With dancing shadows and merry jumps.
I pirouette on roots so wide,
And the ferns giggle — oh, what a ride!

A butterfly lands on my nose,
To chat of petals and flower prose.
'You're lost, my friend, come follow me!'
Said the ladybug, proud as can be.

So off I go, with laughter loud,
The forest my silly, playful shroud.
With dreamy hops and silly spins,
In sunlight's arms, the fun begins!

## The Lushness of Unseen Realms

In the jungle of socks, a treasure does hide,
A map made of twigs, where squirrels confide.
With mushrooms for flags and acorns for gold,
The tales of the forest, forever retold.

A raccoon in shades, he's ready to groove,
Dances with chipmunks, oh, watch them all move!
A canoe made of leaves, drifts down a stream,
In this playful escapade, we dream our big dream.

Beneath the tall oaks, a picnic awaits,
With sandwiches crafted by mischievous mates.
Laughter ensues as the ants join the fun,
Sharing their crumbs under the warm golden sun.

So here in the whimsy, where wild things abound,
An adventure is certain, with joy all around!
The forest's alive with a tickle and tease,
In the lushness of realms, we'll do as we please!

## Reveries of Green-Hearted Wanderers

Oh, the joys of a wander, with butter in tow,
A snail with a hat, oh, where did he go?
With pineapples growing on the high branches tall,
Our laughter erupts as we listen to all.

A cloud of confusion, where lost squirrels roam,
With GPS hidden in a wise bear's home.
Their eyes in a twinkle, they plot and they scheme,
Finding paths to the land of delightful ice cream!

Underneath the blue skies, they wander and play,
Chasing the shadows, not caring the way.
With slapping of paws and a tumble or two,
The green-hearted crew finds the fun in the dew!

So join in the dream, dear forest-bound friend,
Where giggles and wanderings never will end!
With every odd whim, the forest will sing,
Of the mischief and magic that laughter can bring!

## Whispers on Blades of Grass

In the meadows so mellow, where whispers conspire,
The butterflies hum, their electric attire.
They gossip of rumors and tales from the past,
As the laughter of daisies blows gently, at last.

A hedgehog wearing glasses surveys the whole crew,
He's reading old comics while sipping on dew.
With beavers discussing their architectural plans,
They're building a castle with intricate bands!

The giggles of mushrooms go up like a mist,
While crickets compose, they can't be dismissed.
With wind that is chuckling, it tickles the grass,
A whimsical waltz, where the good times will last.

So come with your laughter, come bravely and fast,
In this playful kingdom, let worries be cast!
The blades of green whisper, they're full of delight,
In the land where we frolic, from morning to night!

## Heartbeats of the Woodland

As the owls play poker, their eyes all aglow,
Beneath twinkling stars, they put on quite the show.
A moose with a monocle, oh what a sight!
He wagers with wisdom, by the firelight.

With wind in the branches, the trees start to sway,
They're sharing their secrets in their leafy ballet.
Pine cones roll out like dice on the ground,
In this forest of giggles, the fun can be found.

A badger on drums, with a band of raccoons,
They jive with a vibe that can brighten the moon.
While squirrels on violins play melodies sweet,
The woodland rejoices in this rhythmic beat.

So join all the critters in whimsical glee,
As heartbeats of woodland invite you and me!
In this wild masquerade, we merrily dance,
Leaving traces of laughter in each blooming chance!

## Solace in the Silent Grove

In the grove where shadows play,
Squirrels plot their acorn heist,
Mushrooms dance in disarray,
Nature's chaos, oh so nice!

Birds gossip on a branch so high,
While ants march with a sly parade,
A rabbit's hop, a comical fly,
Oh, what a frolic man-made!

Beneath the trees, I trip and fall,
A root's embrace, a kindred friend,
Laughter echoes, a forest call,
I'll stay, just let the fun extend!

As twilight weaves its misty quilt,
The critters join a wobbly race,
In this silent grove, no guilt,
Just giggles in this wild place!

## **Threads of Time Among the Trees**

Time weaves tales upon the bark,
Whispers rise beneath the leaves,
A squirrel juggles nuts - quite the spark,
While old owls roll their wise sleeves.

My watch says it's time for lunch,
But woodpeckers play tic-tac-toe,
The trees join in with quite the punch,
Who knew they could steal the show?

Lost my path in foliage green,
But a raccoon waves, says 'Hey! Stay!'
I guess this forest is a dream,
Where folly leads and maps dismay.

The sun dips low, a golden thread,
Nature laughs at our brave plans,
With each misstep, new joys spread,
Among the trees, our laughter spans!

## The Allure of the Unseen Trail

A path concealed, a beckoning laugh,
It claims my feet with teasing charms,
A leaf blows by, a crafty staff,
Leading me to mischief's arms.

I strut along with a funny sway,
Tripping over roots like a dance,
The trees chuckle at my display,
They know I'm in for a wild chance.

A hidden brook sings silly tunes,
Frogs join in, quite the jazzy beat,
Fireflies flash like little balloons,
As night falls, we bump up the heat.

With each twist, there's laughter shared,
In the thickets, absurdity reigns,
The unseen trail, fun ensnared,
Where every misstep's a gain!

## Voices of the Verdant Realm

The trees are gossipers, wide and tall,
Their leaves whisper tales of the breeze,
A chipmunk accidentally takes a fall,
While snickering birds share mischief with ease.

Grass tickles toes with playful flair,
As ants march by in a comical line,
I wave to a bear, our silly stare,
In this verdant realm, all's divine!

Branches sway like dancers at a ball,
Frogs croon an offbeat melody,
Each rustle, a giggle, a joyful call,
In the forest, I find my remedy.

As twilight paints the sky with glee,
I join the woodland's merry jest,
Amidst the laughter, I feel so free,
In this realm, I am truly blessed!

## Scent of Earth Through the Canopy

The trees all laugh, their branches sway,
A squirrel dances, what a display!
Mossy socks surround my feet,
As the mushrooms gather for a feast.

Frogs in bow ties begin to croak,
While beetles joke, a funny bloke.
I stumble on roots, a trip and fall,
And hear the forest giggle it all.

The air is filled with scents divine,
Of crispy leaves and fruity wine.
Each step I take, a soft surprise,
A twig snaps, oh how it flies!

I greet the sun, it winks at me,
A playful breeze sings with glee.
A woodland world so lively and bright,
In this jolly place, all feels right.

## The Forest Beckons with Open Arms

A thousand whispers call my name,
The trees are swaying, oh what a game!
Rabbits giggle, a cheeky crowd,
As I join in, I'm feeling proud.

Bears in pajamas roam the lane,
Their fuzzy antics drive me insane!
A raccoon wearing a little hat,
Sure knows how to throw a hat chat.

The flowers gossip with a sway,
Telling tales of a sunny day.
With every step, I trip and laugh,
Nature's humor is quite the craft!

I hug a tree, it hugs me back,
With every quirk, there's joy to unpack.
In this fun abode, I lose the frown,
The forest wears its party crown.

## Nightfall in the Whispering Woods

As dusk descends, the moon makes jest,
Owls in tuxes prepare their best.
The shadows play, a dance so fine,
A humorous twist, like a ballet divine.

Bats in sunglasses swirl by,
While wolves howl at the painted sky.
Crickets play tunes, oh so sweet,
Each chirp and giggle a late-night treat.

Fireflies wink in their glowing suits,
They throw a rave in the leafy roots.
I join the show, but trip on a stone,
The laughter erupts, I'm never alone.

Stars peek down with a twinkling grin,
Messy karaoke, where shenanigans begin.
In the dark, we find our light,
This merry forest feels just right.

## **Footprints of a Dreaming Soul**

In a dreamlike state, I wander wide,
Where puddles laugh and giggles slide.
Bouncing bubbles float with ease,
While raccoons toast to sweet memories.

The ground is soft, like fluffy bread,
I skip and hop, so light, so red.
With every step, I leave behind,
A trail of humor, one of a kind.

Leaves fall down in silly spins,
Whispering secrets of the mischievous wins.
Squirrels roll acorns, having a race,
Their silly puns lit up my face.

Footprints mark where I have been,
With laughter echoing like a dream.
This forest realm, my silly friend,
A whimsical world that never ends.

## The Soul's Thirst for Untamed Spaces

A squirrel in a hat sings on a tree,
Chasing dreams of a world both wild and free.
Pine cones are treasures, nuts are a snack,
As I roam the woods, my pack on my back.

I trip on roots, get tangled in vines,
While pondering if squirrels drink fine wines.
A deer in glasses gives me a wink,
I laugh so hard, I start to think.

Mushrooms dance like they're at a ball,
As leaves mimic confetti, a colorful sprawl.
The brook babbles jokes that make me grin,
In this comedic forest, I always win.

The trees are my audience, clapping away,
With branches outstretched, they cheer and sway.
Nature's circus, where joy has no bounds,
In this lively glade, laughter resounds.

## Between Sunlight and Shadow

The sunbeams spy on creatures below,
While shadows play tag, putting on a show.
A rabbit with style hops in a dance,
Wearing a vest, it takes its chance.

The ferns debate fashion, fronds up high,
While owls in sunglasses just pass by.
A fox with a top hat struts down the lane,
As mushrooms giggle, making quite a stain.

In this oddball realm, everything's a jest,
Where even the rocks have got jokes well-dressed.
The wind whispers secrets that tickle my ear,
As laughter echoes, all worries disappear.

Beneath the sun's gaze, the mischief unfolds,
With friends made of moss and trees, I'm consoled.
A world where giggles weave through the air,
In this sunlight and shadow, I've found my flair.

## Whispers of Forgotten Footpaths

Lost in a maze of whispers and grins,
Where bushes share tales of avocado sins.
A path of pebbles that chuckles and cries,
Laughing at shoes that trip on their ties.

The grass tickles toes as I wander around,
With ants in a march—what humor they've found!
A snail in slow motion, a racecar it seems,
Sprints past my feet, fulfilling its dreams.

A sign says "No dancing," I prance on the rocks,
A bear with a bowtie is counting the clocks.
The tall trees are gossiping, isn't it grand?
In these lost footpaths, we all take a stand.

Every step leads to laughter, each turn a surprise,
In this whimsical realm under cartoonish skies.
For here in the wild, mirth perfectly glows,
In the whispers of nature, silliness flows.

# The Gentle Tug of the Wild

A raccoon in pajamas juggles some crumbs,
While frogs clap their hands, making cheerful drums.
In a meadow of colors, laughter takes flight,
As butterflies join in, dancing in delight.

The grasshoppers hop with a shaky leg stance,
Inviting the bees to join in the dance.
A turtle with swagger pulls off a cool hat,
While nearby, a frog sings like it's all that.

The trees sway like they've had too much fun,
With whispers of mischief from everyone.
A fox with a twist tells the best of the tales,
While owls wink and nod as the humour prevails.

The wild gives a tug, a nudge, and a cheer,
With its playful embrace, I hold my friends near.
In this comedy show where the wilderness strays,
I find my joy in the wild's funny ways.

## A Glimpse of Sunlit Horizons

In the woods where sunbeams play,
Squirrels gossip all the day.
Trees are dancing, roots in tune,
Can you hear the woodpecker's croon?

Mushrooms wear their colors bright,
Frogs are croaking, what a sight!
A deer prances with a grin,
Waving at the raccoons' kin.

The brook babbles jokes so clear,
While the owls give a sly cheer.
Today's the day for frolic and fun,
Who knew the forest could weigh a ton!

As sunlight spills on leafy trails,
The bunnies plot their funny tales.
With laughter echoing through the trees,
Nature giggles in the gentle breeze.

## Dreams Woven in Green Hues

Among the leaves, a shout erupts,
A worm declared he'd won the cups!
With petals soft, they cheer and sway,
    Insects join the grand ballet.

The sun dips low, the shadows stretch,
A bear tries hard to find a sketch.
With every brush and splat of paint,
    The forest's fun, it's never faint!

A bird drops by with jokes anew,
That tickles every pine tree too.
All creatures laugh, then glance above,
    Even the clouds join in the love.

Ferny dreams in colors loud,
The critters paint the forest proud.
With every giggle shared in green,
    Nature's comedic stage is seen.

## The Forest's Hidden Song

Amongst the trees, a tune is born,
The squirrels dance, the birds adorn.
Their quips and quacks, a choral glee,
A symphony of silly spree!

The breeze whispers, 'Dance along!'
With thumping hearts they can't go wrong.
A rabbit prances with great flair,
Inspired by the wind's wild air.

Even the stones begin to roll,
In this soft, playful woodland stroll.
A chipmunk shouts, "Let's sing the blues!"
And echoes bounce in happy hues.

As moonlight glimmers on the way,
They giggle softly, ending day.
The forest hums its hidden song,
Where laughter stirs and dreams belong.

## Nature's Breath in Quiet Valleys

In valleys where the whispers sneak,
The flowers giggle, "Come and peek!"
With bees in bowties, they all twirl,
Nature's ball, a wacky whirl.

A rock claims it's the king of hills,
While fog shares all its morning thrills.
Tadpoles flaunt their little ways,
As brambles chuckle, "What a gaze!"

The sunbeams play a hide and seek,
With shadows jumping, oh so sleek.
Each gust of wind tells a joke,
While trees weave memories with oak.

When twilight dances, colors blend,
The owls hoot just to make amends.
In quiet valleys, joy does bloom,
Nature's breath sings laughs that loom.

## Journey Through Verdant Veils

In a green land where squirrels plot,
A raccoon steals snacks with a sly little trot.
Branches tickle, laughter fills the air,
Was that a gnome? I'm not quite aware.

A pinecone falls, hits me on the head,
I blame the trees, for this mischief widespread.
Elves in the shadows wink with delight,
Sipping on nectar while I itch and swipe.

A deer prances by, antlers askew,
It takes one look, then giggles too.
Whispers surround, it's a forest plot,
An avenue of antics I never thought.

Each step reveals secrets, each path a jest,
Nature's a comedian; I'm merely a guest.
In shadows and sun, life dances with glee,
Who knew the woods were this funny, and free?

## Secrets of the Shadowed Grove

Beneath the shadows where laughter hides,
A hedgehog dances on the woodland slides.
Owls hoot in giggles, watch closely they stare,
While mushrooms gossip about the local fare.

A fox plays tricks, with a mischievous grin,
Telling tall tales of where he's been.
Moss-covered stones chuckle with grace,
As I trip and tumble, it's a slapstick race.

The canopy sways, tickling my nose,
Trust me, these boughs are comical pros.
They tease and they tease with every sway,
In this silly zone, I'm the punchline today.

I hear twig giggles as I pass through,
"Careful!" they say, "Or we'll trip you too!"
In a nature sitcom, I'm the star of the show,
With trees as my backup, putting on quite the show!

# The Enchantment of Green Horizons

In emerald hues, the world sings bright,
Dance with the leaves, let's take flight!
A snail in a hurry, or so it would seem,
Races elite, for the leaf-hopping dream.

Frogs croak rhythms, a quirky old band,
I tap my feet, not quite as planned.
The breeze plays jokes with my tangled hair,
Caught in the fun without a care!

Sunbeams play tricks, kissing my cheek,
It's all just a joke that nature will tweak.
A butterfly lands, flips me the wing,
In this crazy land, the forest can sing.

Pine needles fall like confetti in cheer,
Around every tree, there's laughter to hear.
With each step I take, I join in the play,
In this green oblivion, I'm lost in a sway.

# A Tapestry of Timbered Tales

Whispers of woodlands flit through the air,
Where trees share their secrets, it's never a scare.
A beaver's build is quite the joke,
"Why not a lodge?" he quips, "No need for smoke!"

Foxes swap fables of daring delight,
Slip-ups and pratfalls, all taking flight.
The breeze chuckles softly, trailing behind,
In comedy's clutch, I have to unwind.

The sun sets a stage, where shadows do dance,
Nature's soirée, not leaving to chance.
Mushrooms parade, in polka-dot lines,
While crickets provide the night's funny signs.

Giggles ensue as a twig snaps in haste,
Every nook holds a secret—a chuckle, a taste.
In the tapestry woven with mischief and cheer,
These tales of the timber will always endear.

# Adventures Among Spiraling Roots

In a land where the trees twist and twirl,
I tripped on a root, gave the ground a whirl.
A squirrel giggled, held a nut like a prize,
While I danced around with surprise in my eyes.

Branches whispered secrets, rustled with glee,
I followed a path that led straight to a bee.
But the bee was a diva, it buzzed like a star,
And I ducked in the bushes, like it knew who we are.

Leaves chuckled softly, a tickle on cheek,
They waved at my clumsiness, oh, what a peek!
Underfoot mushrooms formed a wacky parade,
Then stumbled upon a toad who had serenades.

With all my missteps, I started to grin,
At nature's own circus, I felt like a win.
Among spiraling roots, I learned with delight,
That laughter in forests can be pure, just right.

## Memories Captured in Dappled Light

Sunbeams danced lightly, a polka with cheer,
While I chased golden shadows, wishing for beer.
A raccoon played tricks, with eyes full of jest,
As I tried to catch rays that thought they were best.

Fallen leaves giggled, rustling quiet tunes,
As I waved to the mushrooms with wide-eyed cartoons.
A lizard made faces, bizarre and so sly,
It twisted and turned, with a wink of an eye.

All the memories sparkled, like fireflies' flight,
I stumbled on laughter, beneath the soft light.
With every step taken, a new snapshot drawn—
Dappled was life; I was happily on!

Caught in a moment, forever I'll be,
With stories of sunshine and roots that run free.
For in nature's embrace, every giggle takes flight,
And memories linger, all captured in light.

## **Lost Amongst the Elder Boughs**

I wandered too far, where shadows collide,
Amongst ancient giants, I turned for a ride.
Twisted trails tangled like spaghetti on trees,
And whispering branches played tricks with the breeze.

An owl wore glasses, reading rustic old books,
While a hedgehog in sneakers gave me curious looks.
'You're lost,' it exclaimed, rolling into a ball,
As I laughed at my map that led me to fall.

Fungi held council with caps oh so grand,
Conspiring, perhaps, to lead me offhand.
Through elder boughs swaying, wisdom was shared,
And I giggled aloud at the fun that I dared.

Finally, moonlit, I stumbled on home,
With tales of the forest, where wild things roam.
In the heart of such chaos, I found glee like no other,
There's joy in getting lost, oh, nature, my brother!

## **Where the Foliage Holds Secrets**

Beneath leafy arches, the secrets abound,
Whispers of squirrels spin tales from the ground.
A chipmunk wore boots; it strutted with flair,
While I attempted a leap, landed flat on my hair.

The whispers were giggles that tickled the trees,
While butterflies flitted on zephyrs with ease.
Amidst leafy roars, a hedgehog went past,
With a monocle on, calling life quite a blast.

Branches were gossiping, sharing a jest,
As I tripped on a root, going east instead west.
The foliage roared with laughter so loud,
As I blushed into blooms, feeling quite proud.

I discovered a patch where mushrooms all swayed,
In a conga line cadence, their jubilee played.
So, if you find merriment under the trees,
Remember, in nature, it's laughter that frees!

## The Silence Between the Trunks

In a woodland so grand, there's a faint laugh,
A squirrel named Chuck gives the trees a gaffe.
He hides all the acorns beneath the tall pines,
Plotting his heist while the forest declines.

The breeze whispers secrets to bushes ahead,
While Chuck, oh so clever, dreams of his bread.
He burrows for snacks where the daisies grow,
Who knew forest feasts come with such a glow?

Underneath the broad limbs, his treasure he finds,
Fall chases the sun, and he ponders new designs.
A party for critters, a banquet of nuts,
Just need a few mushrooms—oh, but they spout guts!

Yet in all of this chaos, serenity blooms,
Every root, every branch, hosts myriad costumes.
Laughter erupts, as they dance and they prance,
In this humor-filled forest, there's always a chance.

## Shadows Stretching at Dusk

As daylight takes off, and shadows get sassy,
A chipmunk named Timmy begins to get classy.
He dons a small hat, a bow tie, oh my!
Preparing for night when the moon's in the sky.

The owls in their wisdom start hooting with glee,
As Timmy declares, "Come, join the party with me!"
The shadows are shifting, a waltz of delight,
In this whimsy of dusk, everything feels right.

With crickets on violins, they all take a stand,
Turns out forest folk are the best music band.
The trees sway and chuckle, joining the scene,
In this twilight cabaret, all's cozy and keen.

With laughter and giggles, they dance 'neath the stars,
Timmy stumbles, but nobody cares about scars.
As shadows stretch longer, their antics don't wane,
In this twilight of cheer, there's nothing but gain.

## Essence of Wildflowers and Sunbeams

Among blooms so vibrant, where sunlight will peek,
A bee named Sir Buzz is quite bold and unique.
He flirts with each flower, in yellow he buzzs,
Claiming that nature has more friends than it does.

With petals like dresses, the daisies all cheer,
For nobody wants to end up a mere sphere.
They dance 'round the bee, making fragrance with grace,
In this fragrant affair, they all find their place.

But oh, the mischief, as Sir Buzz takes a dive,
Into all the sweet nectar, where bees really thrive.
He channels his bravery, one sip leads to two,
Now he's wobbly-flying—not sure what to do!

The flowers giggle softly, their laughter so sweet,
As he zigzags around, trying hard not to meet,
A bumblebee's burden is a fun life, it seems,
In a sunbeam's embrace, they fulfill all their dreams.

## Voices of the Elusive Wilderness

In a glen where the wild things hold all their meetings,
A rabbit named Rory discusses high greetings.
With eyes wide and twitching, he states his grand plan:
To build a fine home for the whole critter clan.

The squirrels roll laughter from branches so tight,
Countless old stories come alive in the night.
With voices resounding, they share jokes and gags,
Spreading cheer through the woods—and all of their swags.

A raccoon joins in with a tip of his hat,
"Listen here, everyone, it's all just chit-chat!
We share and we play, in this wilderness free,
Where nature's our stage, and we're all meant to be!"

So in rustling whispers that carry on air,
They celebrate life with a woodland flair.
For among all the joys and the ruckus and fun,
The voices of nature sing loud as a gun.

## Twilights Drenched in Green Light

In the hush of leaves, a squirrel grins,
Winks at the moon, as the evening spins.
A raccoon in a mask, oh what a sight,
Dances with shadows, under soft light.

They gather for tea, in mossy retreat,
With cups made of acorns, so dainty and neat.
The owl serves the cake, with a wise little nod,
While fireflies debate, who's the best rod.

A bear in pajamas, just rolled out of bed,
Complains about twigs, he stepped on instead.
"Where's the real buffet?" he heartily roars,
"Not this leafy salad, I need s'more scores!"

As twilight settles, the giggles spread wide,
Nature's own party, with chaos as pride.
In a world where the creatures can throw quite a fuss,
We laugh at their antics and join in the truss.

**Echoes of the Forest's Heart**

From branches above, comes a raucous cheer,
As woodpeckers drum, they go, "Can you hear?"
A chorus of chirps, a whimsical show,
With frogs croaking bass to set the tempo.

A moose in a tux, what a dapper display,
Claims he's the king of the forest ballet.
Goes to the pond, flipping his tail,
While rabbits critique, "He's got to work pale!"

Through the conifers tall, a wild caper trails,
As foxes in sneakers, tell tall tales.
"Did you hear of the badger who learned to moonwalk?"
They giggle, they snicker, as they start to talk.

Under the starlit glimmer, it's quite the delight,
With jesters in fur, making jokes every night.
Nature's own laughter, echoes so clear,
In this woodland theatre, full of good cheer.

## Secrets Veiled by Fog

In the misty morn, a parrot proclaims,
"I'm 'lost' in the fog, but it's all part of games!"
He flaps and he flails, in a fit of applause,
While raccoons play hide, with sneaky little jaws.

A ghostly old tree, whispers secrets untold,
Of acorns that shimmer, and mushrooms quite bold.
But a curious bunny, peers in with a grin,
Says, "Spill the beans, we're all eager to win!"

With each whisper dawn's light, begins to unfold,
Where laughter and fog mix, in the chill of the gold.
A hedgehog with glasses, reading the news,
Says, "Hey! Play it straight, or face the big blues!"

The shadows recede, as the giggles take flight,
Those forest tales woven, with pure-hearted fright.
In the fog, they confide, where mischief awaits,
As the trees laugh along, at their curious fates.

## Treasures Found in Nature's Arms

In the depths of the thicket, treasures abound,
A sock left by someone, covers all ground.
The frogs croak a tune, while the snails draw the map,
As beetles hold court, with a well-timed clap.

Golden leaves scattered, like coins in the creek,
"Found fortune!" bellows a fox with a squeak.
"Pay up!" says a squirrel, with a twinkle in eye,
As he counts all the acorns, stacked high in a pile.

A thistle dons crowns, for a royal parade,
Bees buzz about, for a honey trade.
"Roll out the carpet, it's beggars and kings!"
They dance through the woods, on their shimmering wings.

In this cradle of whimsy, where laughter runs wild,
Nature's a jester, and we are the child.
So let's gather our treasures and share with all fun,
For in this green laughter, our hearts become one.

## Echoes of Untamed Dreams

Whispers of trees giggle above,
Squirrels in hats, what a sight of love.
Bumbling bears dance to the breeze,
While owls ask for snacks—oh, please!

Frogs in tuxedos jump to the beat,
Chasing their tails on their tiny feet.
Rabbits play tag, but who's it now?
Each laugh echoing through the boughs.

## The Lure of Moss-Covered Trails


Mossy paths beg for a stroll,
With mushrooms wearing hats—how droll!
In this green nook, giggles abound,
Even the mushrooms engage in sound.

A toad on a log plays the flute,
While crickets chirp in pursuit.
It's a scene from a bizarre play,
Where forest creatures laugh all day.

## Secrets of the Shadowed Grove

In shadows, secrets twist and twine,
Raccoons as spies, plotting divine.
They whisper secrets with a wink,
"Let's hide a carrot!"—what do you think?

A fox in sneakers runs with flair,
Dodging sneaky birds in mid-air.
The trees might giggle, creaking low,
As antics unfold in this wild show.

## Lost in the Lush Embrace

In a tangle where silliness reigns,
Bears slip on branches, ignoring the pains.
They giggle and tumble, what a parade,
While flowers laugh, in wild masquerade.

Brambles tease with thorns in disguise,
But laughter erupts, loud as the skies.
With each stumble and fall, they sing,
In this embrace, joy's the only king.

## **Lullabies of Leaves in the Wind**

Whispers of leaves in a giggly breeze,
Swaying to tunes of buzzing bees.
Trees wear hats made of moss, so bright,
Tickling the clouds in a playful flight.

The squirrels dance with a wiggly flair,
Juggling acorns without a care.
Rabbits hop in a fuzzy parade,
Waving their paws, all mischief displayed.

A cuckoo sings while twirling 'round,
Expecting applause from the ground.
With each ribbit, frogs jest their fate,
Telling their tales at a greeny gate.

So laugh with the forest, in leafy glee,
Join the whimsy of nature's spree.
In this woodland carnival, pure delight,
Where giggles and rustles dance through the night.

## Secrets of the Age-Worn Trees

Old trees gossip in deep, croaky tones,
Sharing their secrets with weathered stones.
A wise owl notes down every joke,
While a startled raccoon dodges the smoke.

Branches contort into silly shapes,
Like a gingerbread man caught in the drapes.
Once a tree, now a bench of dreams,
Where owlets practice their comic routines.

The roots tickle the critters below,
Launching them lightly with each little blow.
A woodpecker laughs at the giggles near,
As echoes of joy dance through every ear.

Ancient bark tells tales with a grin,
Of youthful romps and mischievous sins.
In the heart of the grove, laughter will fill,
Nature's own comedy, a whimsical thrill.

## Ephemeral Moments in Verdant Dreams

In sun-dappled glades, the shadows play,
As ladybugs roll in the foliage's sway.
Fireflies blink like tiny stage lights,
Setting the mood for hilariously bright nights.

A dancing fern twirls with glee,
While beetles host a grand jamboree.
A toad croaks out a ribbeting joke,
Making turtles chuckle till they choke.

Mushrooms wiggle, in pirouetting delight,
Painting the forest in luminous sight.
Winds whistle notes of a mirthful rhyme,
Tickling the leaves, keeping perfect time.

In these fleeting moments, laughter's the weft,
Stitching together the joy we've heft.
So embrace the whimsy in nature's schemes,
Savoring smiles in our verdant dreams.

## Journeys Between the Trees

Venturing forth where the wild things trot,
A parade of critters, oh what a lot!
Chipmunks wear hats made of dandelion fluff,
Acting like kings, oh isn't that tough?

Branches become bridges in the sunny expanse,
Where shadows and sunlight giggle and dance.
A snail on a quest, with no rush at all,
Confidently heads to the old water stall.

Through thickets and brambles, a raucous trail,
Chasing adventures, both silly and frail.
With every rustle, comes forth a new tune,
Nature itself, like a jester, is strewn.

So roam with the laughter that beckons so clear,
In journeys where folly overrules fear.
Amongst the tall giants, life's humor unfolds,
In paths of green laughter, where mystery beholds.

## Echoes of the Sylvan Spirit

In the woods where squirrels dance,
A chipmunk's got a second chance.
He dropped his nut, oh what a sight,
  It rolled away and took to flight.

The trees they giggle, roots all grin,
Kicking up leaves, let the fun begin.
  A raccoon wears a tiny hat,
It's quite the fashion - imagine that!

## Footsteps in the Fern's Embrace

Wandering through a ferny maze,
I trip on roots, a clumsy phase.
A babbling brook starts to chuckle,
I join the laugh, though it's a struggle.

A deer prances by, a graceful tease,
It snorts like it just discovered cheese.
With twigs in hair, I make my way,
The forest knows, it's just a play.

## The Comfort of Canopied Solitude

Under leaves, I lay quite flat,
Dreaming of goldfish, oh imagine that!
A crow caws loud, a funny banshee,
Says, "Get up! Go climb that tree!"

The hammock sways, a cozy swoop,
And brings my snack - a squirrel troop.
With acorns tossed, they run around,
I laugh aloud, oh such a sound!

## Memories Hidden in the Brambles

Thorns are hairy, brambles poke,
Caught in laughter, I try to choke.
It's a tangle of days gone past,
Where stories live, and laughs hold fast.

A hedgehog rolls with such great flair,
In his own world, without a care.
The forest whispers, "Life's a play,"
I'm just the star of this wild array!

## Where Fables Meet the Ferns

In a glade where tales run wild,
Ferns whisper secrets, oh so mild.
A squirrel debates with a wise old crow,
And they giggle at humans who just don't know.

Mice throw a party, the cheese is grand,
While raccoons play poker, oh what a stand!
The owl hoots loudly, claiming the night,
While rabbits jump in, bursting with delight.

Trees share stories of days long past,
Of knights and dragons, they had a blast.
But the best part is, no one will tell,
Who really won the game of hide and yell!

As dawn approaches, tales fade away,
Yet laughter lingers, come what may.
A quick note jotted on a leaf of thyme,
Next week we'll meet for another good time!

## The Lure of Hidden Clearings

In a clearing, the sun plays peek-a-boo,
With the stumps and logs, where mushrooms grew.
Fairies with wings of glimmering zest,
Compete in a race, it's all in good jest.

A frog in a top hat performs a grand show,
While crickets keep rhythm, putting on a faux glow.
The hedgehogs beat drums made of scattered twigs,
And hold a wild dance that brightens their digs.

"I swear that tree moved!" a squirrel will shout,
While the mushrooms giggle, with no hint of doubt.
The bumblebees buzz like a live rock band,
As nature laughs hard, it is all quite unplanned.

When twilight approaches, the moon takes its seat,
Moonlight's confetti makes everything sweet.
They toast with acorns, the party's a hit,
In the hidden clearing, everyone fits!

## **Footsteps on Forgotten Trails**

In shadows where signs of time grow dim,
Footsteps tickle the twigs with a playful whim.
Lost in the giggles of rustling leaves,
Where even the lost come just to tease.

A wandering bear in search of a snack,
Dances like no one's watching, no sense to hold back.
Roots trip a few, giving nature a laugh,
And the birds chime in, what a joyful gaffe!

Abandoned paths tell tales of the past,
Where every twist and turn is a comical cast.
Why did the chicken cross preposterous streams?
To join in the mischief of whimsical dreams!

With every step, a chuckle, a stumble,
Nature's mishaps, so easy to fumble.
Yet through all the giggles, one truth rings clear,
Adventure awaits for those without fear!

## Serenade of the Sylvan Breeze

In the arms of trees, where whispers combine,
The breeze sings a tune, oh so divine.
Laughter rings out, it swirls through the air,
As nature holds parties, beyond all compare.

A dandy old fox in a vest of bright hues,
Tells tales of lost socks and runaway shoes.
The rabbits compose a playful ballet,
While the owls debate which word to convey.

Every gust carries giggles, oh what a show,
The leaves shimmy and sway, put on a glow.
The sun beams so bright, it's hard to believe,
How much fun these woods can weave and retrieve.

As twilight arrives, the stars seem to jest,
"You think you're alone? Come join the fest!"
Under the moon's watchful, twinkling embrace,
Every night in the forest is a grand, funny place!

## **The Embrace of Ancient Roots**

In tangled vines, I trip and fall,
I swear the trees have seen it all.
They laugh at me with leafy grins,
As squirrels plan their next set of wins.

With roots that grab my wandering feet,
It's hard to dance to this forest beat.
The branches wave, a playful tease,
While I just try to find the breeze.

Mossy blankets hug my toes tight,
As shadows dance in morning light.
A gnarled oak cracks a wise old joke,
I giggle back, and we both choke.

Oh ancient roots, you're quite the friend,
But please don't trip me, it's hard to mend.
With every step, I hear you boast,
Next time, I'll bring my forest ghost.

## Reflections in the Misty Glade

In a glade where the fog swirls wide,
I trip on a root, take a graceless slide.
The trees all snicker as I flail,
While frogs just croak their humorous tale.

The mirror pond reflects my fright,
With goofy faces in morning light.
A deer looks on with a raised brow,
"Is that a dancer? Oh, someone tell how!"

I splash and splash, it can't be true,
The fish are laughing! Oh, how rude!
I twirl like leaves in a sudden gust,
And hope my forest skills become a must.

But what is this, a rabbit's cheer?
He hops with joy, "Come laugh with me here!"
We bounce around in a merry show,
And leave behind all thoughts of woe.

# A Quest for the Wild Unknown

I set out boldly with snacks in hand,
To uncover secrets of this wild land.
The compass spins, it must be broken,
As nature whispers more than it's spoken.

A babbling brook begins to chat,
"Don't follow that path, it's a bad hat!"
My map, it crinkles under my gaze,
Turns out I've wandered a likely maze.

A raccoon pops out, says, "What's for lunch?"
"Uh-oh!" I stammer, dodging a punch.
He offers me berries, a wild delight,
But they leave me hopping through the night.

With each wrong turn, I learn to jest,
"Next time, I'll let the GPS do the quest!"
I'll never doubt that I can roam,
With giggles and snacks, nature feels like home.

## Tales Told by the Wind

The wind comes in with a playful shout,
"Did you hear what the owls are about?"
They share their tales with a hoot and a wink,
While I laugh hard, too busy to think.

The breeze wraps round like an old friend's hug,
"Why not try the dance of the ladybug?"
I twirl on a leaf, it's quite the sight,
As acorns roll by in a lazy flight.

"Oh look!" the trees yell, "a scampering hare!
He's tripped on a branch, don't you dare stare!"
Laughter echoes through every bough,
As I join in, feeling light as a cow.

With whispers and giggles from nature's choir,
Each gust of wind takes me higher and higher.
I'll tell these tales by the firelight glow,
Of silly dances and forest friends in tow.

## **Breath of the Ancient Trees**

Whispers of leaves tickle my ears,
Mighty trunks hold secrets and cheers.
Squirrels plot with mischief in mind,
While owls roll their eyes, oh so unkind.

A raccoon with snacks steals my heart,
Waving his paws, he plays the part.
Branches sway in the dance of delight,
Nature's jesters, oh what a sight!

## The Spirit of the Undergrowth

In the shadows, a mossy prankster,
Fungi giggle as I become a wankster.
Rabbits play hopscotch in the mud,
While I trip over roots like a thud.

Dancing shadows with a cheeky grin,
Tickled by ferns, am I wearing thin?
Beneath the brambles, laughter is found,
As I tumble and roll on the ground.

## **Paths Uncharted**

Lost in a maze, I twist and I twirl,
A squirrel watches my awkward swirl.
Twigs crack beneath my clumsy tread,
Echoes of laughter dance in my head.

The compass spins like a game of charades,
With each turn, I find new cascades.
Mushrooms nod in approval, so sly,
As I wander under the watchful sky.

**Souls Untethered**

The breeze blows softly, a tickling touch,
While fairies giggle just out of clutch.
Blades of grass whisper secrets untold,
As I dance with bugs, feeling bold.

Hands reach for the sky, I leap and I spin,
Blissfully clueless, it's a quirky win.
In the company of trees, I find my beat,
Together we waltz, how ridiculously sweet!

## A Reverie Among the Roots

Laying low, I play peek-a-boo,
With butterflies and ants, oh, who knew?
Roots entwined like a jolly parade,
Each a tale that the earth has made.

In wild reverie, my thoughts take flight,
Chasing shadows that dance in the light.
Oh, to be a twig in this comic refrain,
Living in laughter, embracing the bane!

## **Tenderness of the Trilling Birds**

In the tree tops, they squawk and sing,
A concert of chirps, oh what a fling!
With feathers all ruffled, they flaunt their style,
Nestled in branches, they gossip a while.

When one takes a dive, it's quite the sight,
Flapping all wildly, they give quite a fright.
With beaks full of berries, they wobble and sway,
Forever amusing us, day after day.

## Embrace of the Endless Green.

The leaves look like hands waving hello,
While branches shake back in a friendly flow.
A squirrel darting, such speed to admire,
As acorns rain down, their own little choir.

Every splash of sunlight breeds giggles and cheer,
With shadows that dance, sneaking up from the rear.
Oh, the grass tickles toes, what a silly delight,
In the warm, leafy arms, we skip through the light.

## Wandering Whispers of the Woods

Mossy carpets hide secrets untold,
While the wise old trees are brimming with gold.
Frogs in a chorus, croaking in tune,
While chipmunks plot mischief under the moon.

Roots twist like noodles, a strange tangled dance,
With nature's odd humor, it's hard not to prance.
Whispers of critters lead us astray,
Yet we stumble on laughter, come what may!

### **Enchanted Paths Beneath the Canopy.**

Beneath leafy arches, we wander with glee,
As fireflies giggle, oh can't you just see?
With every loose branch that hangs in our way,
We dodge and weave like we're in a ballet.

Squirrels are critiquing our formidable style,
As owls hoot approval, sporting wise smiles.
The ground's a trampoline for more than just feet,
With laughter echoing, life's, oh so sweet!

## Fables Hidden in the Underbrush

A squirrel reads tales on a mushroom cap,
While a fox sips tea from a tiny nap.
The owl can't stop laughing, it's quite absurd,
As the rabbit rushes by, saying, 'Have you heard?'

Beneath the brambles, stories take flight,
With gingerbread houses hidden from sight.
The hedgehog is knitting with twigs and some moss,
While the raccoon declares, 'I am the boss!'

In the thicket, secrets peek out to say,
That gnomes do their laundry by half-light of day.
But the wind tells the stories, with giggles and hums,
As it tickles the tree trunks, and all nature drums.

Their whispers entice in the wild, lovely game,
While the grasshoppers hop in, just feeding the fame.
Through laughter and leaves, the fables will roam,
In this silly old forest, we all call our home.

## Serpentine Trails of Wonder

Down winding paths where the mushrooms dance,
A turtle in goggles takes quite a chance.
His snail friend is yawning, missed all the fun,
'How slow can you go?' they joked on the run.

A parrot recounts tales, dressed up as a knight,
While the crickets provide a sweet symphonic night.
The raccoons performed a rather grand show,
As owls hooted loud, putting on quite the glow.

Beneath tangled vines, they find treasures galore,
With acorns as jewels, they add to their store.
The forest chuckles, with branches that sway,
Dancing shadows telling jokes until the next day.

As they wander the curves, their laughter takes flight,
Chasing shadows at dusk, they're seen in moonlight.
With snickers and giggles, the serpents will twist,
A party in nature no critter can resist.

## Journey's End in the Arboreal Realm

At the end of the trail, where the pine trees chat,
A hedgehog declares, 'I'm not scared of that!'
The beaver builds hats out of leaves to sell,
While the chipmunks plot how to ring the bell.

The trees gossip low, with whispers so sweet,
About a raccoon hopping on oversized feet.
He trips on a root, does a hilarious spin,
While the crowd of the forest lets the giggles begin.

Squirrels throw acorns as confetti in cheer,
Welcoming all creatures that dare to come near.
The moonlight invites for a ball in the glade,
Where the laughter of critters is happily made.

When the journey concludes with a dance and a clap,
In this merry old wood, there's just no need for a map.
With smiles and delight, under starlit expanse,
They sing for their neighbors in a whimsical dance.

## Beneath the Stars and Sycamores

Beneath sycamore arms, under winks of the night,
The fireflies twinkle, a flickering light.
A fox tells tall tales of his daring plight,
While badgers all giggle, with eyes open wide.

In pajamas of bark, a raccoon combs his fur,
While crickets are chorusing, making a stir.
A weasel does cartwheels, impresses in style,
As the owls shake their heads at the antics awhile.

The stars play peekaboo through the leafy green,
Showing off wonders, a magical scene.
The forest is buzzing with laughter and pranks,
While the frogs play on harps made of twigs in their ranks.

As night gives a nod, and the laughter does sway,
In the glimmer of joy, the woodlands can play.
So if you should wander, take heed of the fun,
Under stars and sycamores, the world's never done.